THE HINDENBURG DISASTER

BY CHRIS BOWMAN
ILLUSTRATION BY BRENT SCHOONOVER
COLOR BY GERARDO SANDOVAL

BELLWETHER MEDIA · MINNEAPOLIS, MN

Black Sheep

STRAY FROM REGULAR READS WITH BLACK SHEEP BOOKS. FEEL A RUSH WITH EVERY READ!

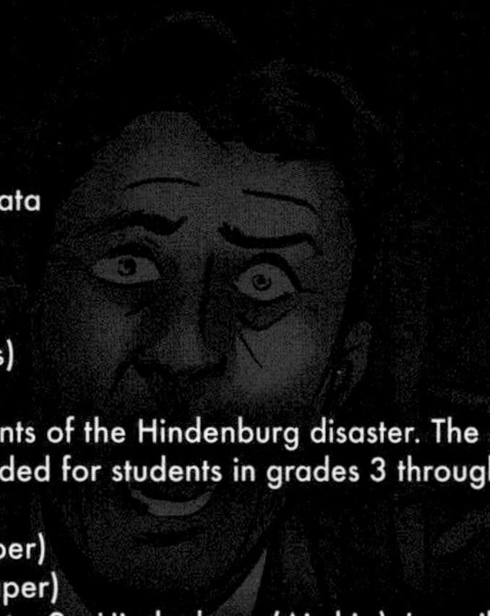

Library of Congress Cataloging-in-Publication Data

Bowman, Chris, 1990-
The Hindenburg Disaster / by Chris Bowman.
pages cm. – (Black Sheep: Disaster Stories)
Includes bibliographical references and index.
Summary: "Exciting illustrations follow the events of the Hindenburg disaster. The combination of brightly colored panels and leveled text is intended for students in grades 3 through 7"– Provided by publisher.
ISBN 978-1-62617-153-4 (hardcover : alk. paper)
ISBN 978-1-62617-522-8 (paperback : alk. paper)
1. Hindenburg (Airship)–Comic books, strips, etc. 2. Hindenburg (Airship)–Juvenile literature. 3. Aircraft accidents–New Jersey–Comic books, strips, etc. 4. Aircraft accidents–New Jersey–Juvenile literature. 5. Airships–Germany–Comic books, strips, etc. 6. Airships–Germany–Juvenile literature. I. Title.
TL659.H5B69 2014
363.12′492–dc23
2014009046

This edition first published in 2016 by Bellwether Media, Inc.

Printed in the United States of America, North Mankato, MN.

TABLE OF CONTENTS

Orange text identifies
historical quotes.

A Smooth Beginning

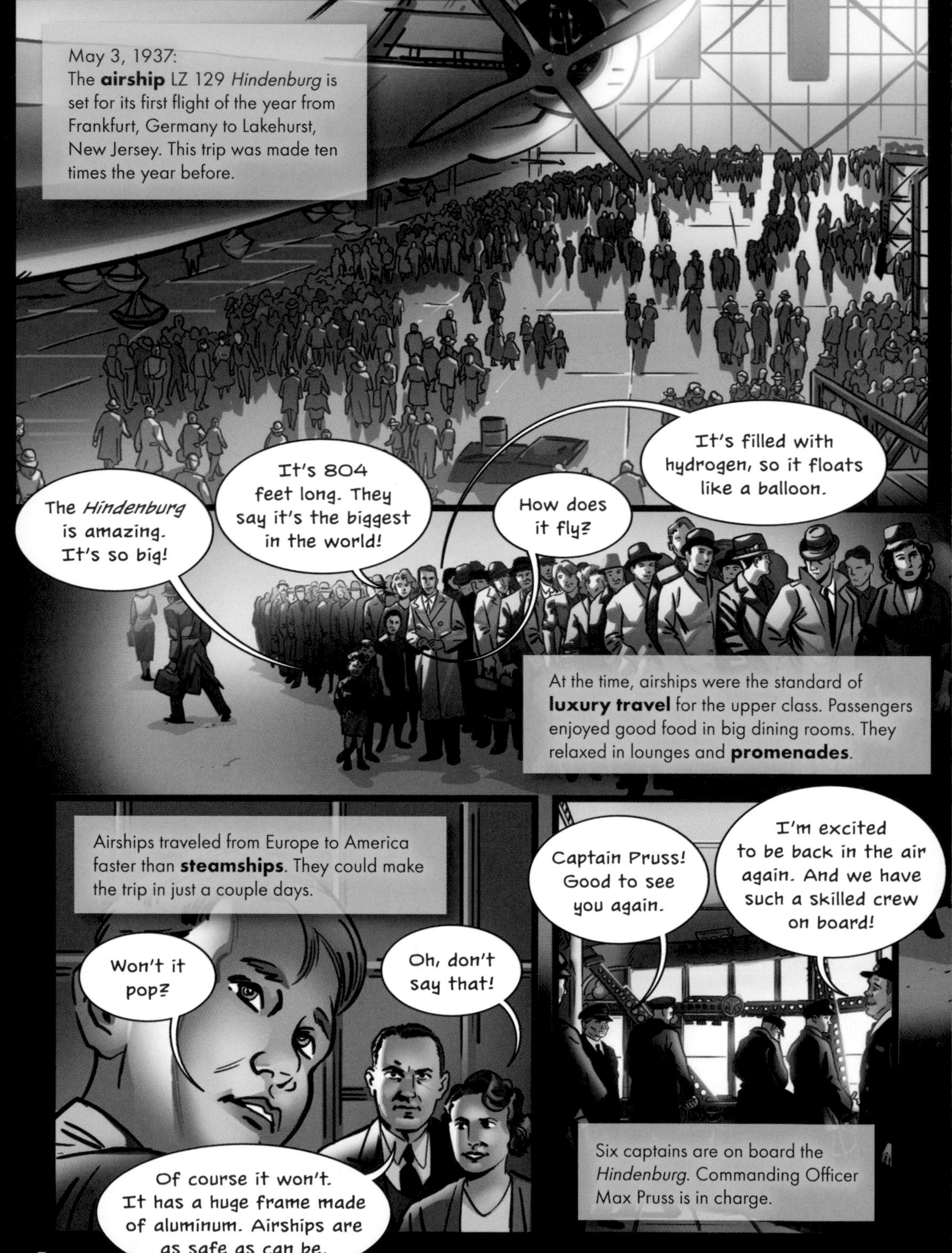

May 3, 1937:
The **airship** LZ 129 *Hindenburg* is set for its first flight of the year from Frankfurt, Germany to Lakehurst, New Jersey. This trip was made ten times the year before.
The *Hindenburg* is amazing. It's so big!
It's 804 feet long. They say it's the biggest in the world!
How does it fly?
It's filled with hydrogen, so it floats like a balloon.
At the time, airships were the standard of **luxury travel** for the upper class. Passengers enjoyed good food in big dining rooms. They relaxed in lounges and **promenades**.
Airships traveled from Europe to America faster than **steamships**. They could make the trip in just a couple days.
Won't it pop?
Oh, don't say that!
Of course it won't. It has a huge frame made of aluminum. Airships are as safe as can be.
Captain Pruss! Good to see you again.
I'm excited to be back in the air again. And we have such a skilled crew on board!
Six captains are on board the *Hindenburg*. Commanding Officer Max Pruss is in charge.

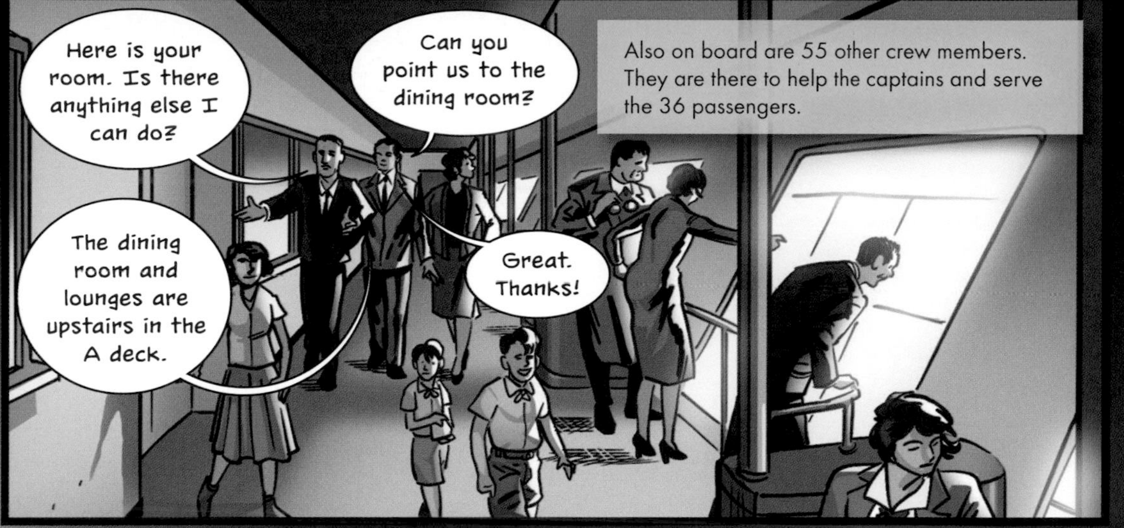
Here is your room. Is there anything else I can do?
Can you point us to the dining room?
Also on board are 55 other crew members. They are there to help the captains and serve the 36 passengers.
The dining room and lounges are upstairs in the A deck.
Great. Thanks!

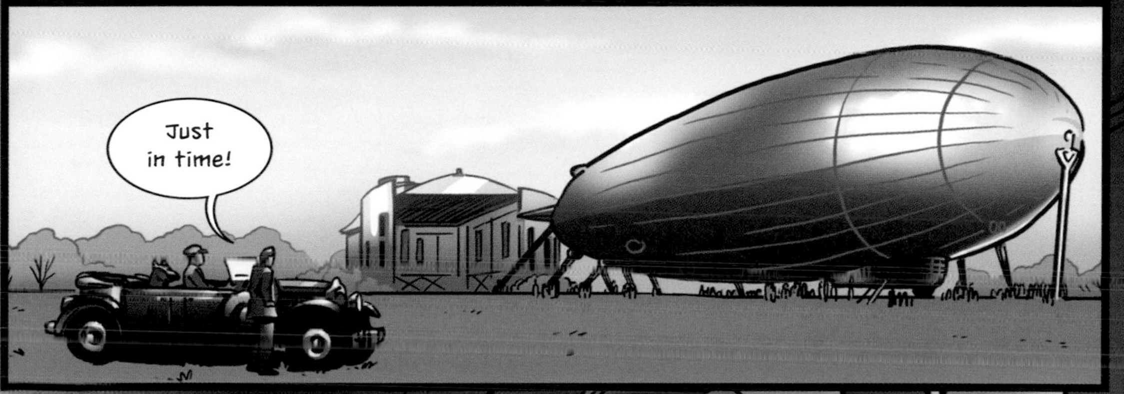
Just in time!

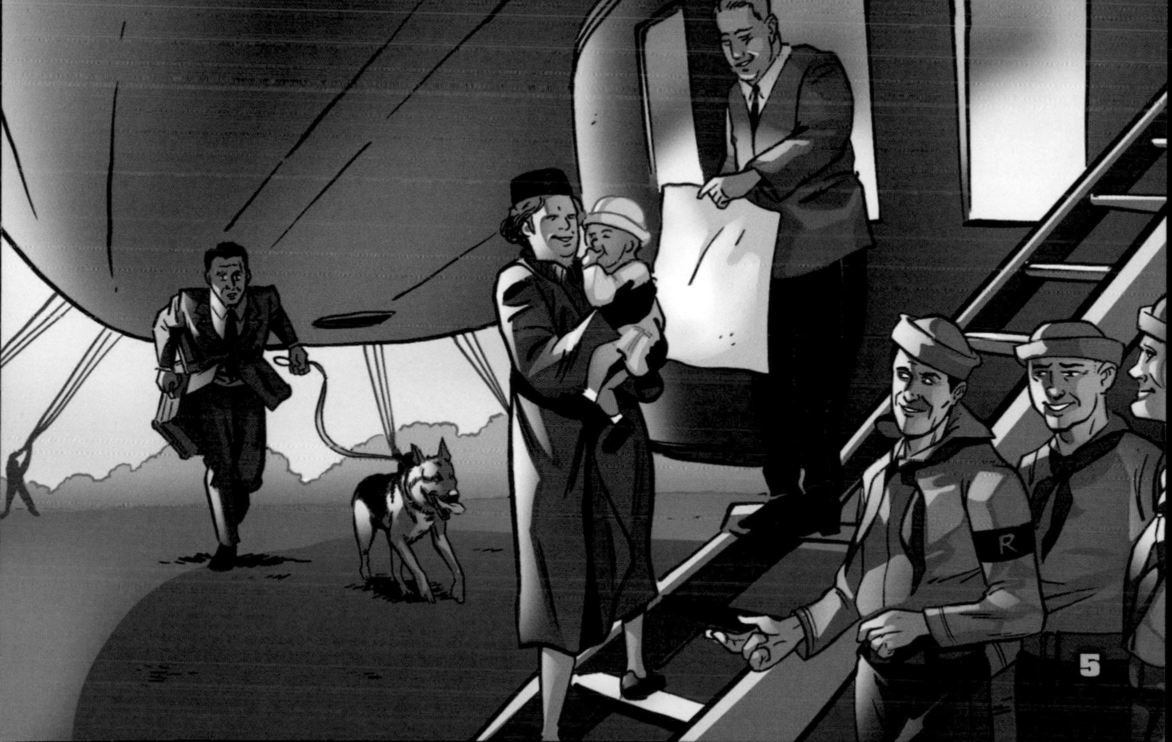
R

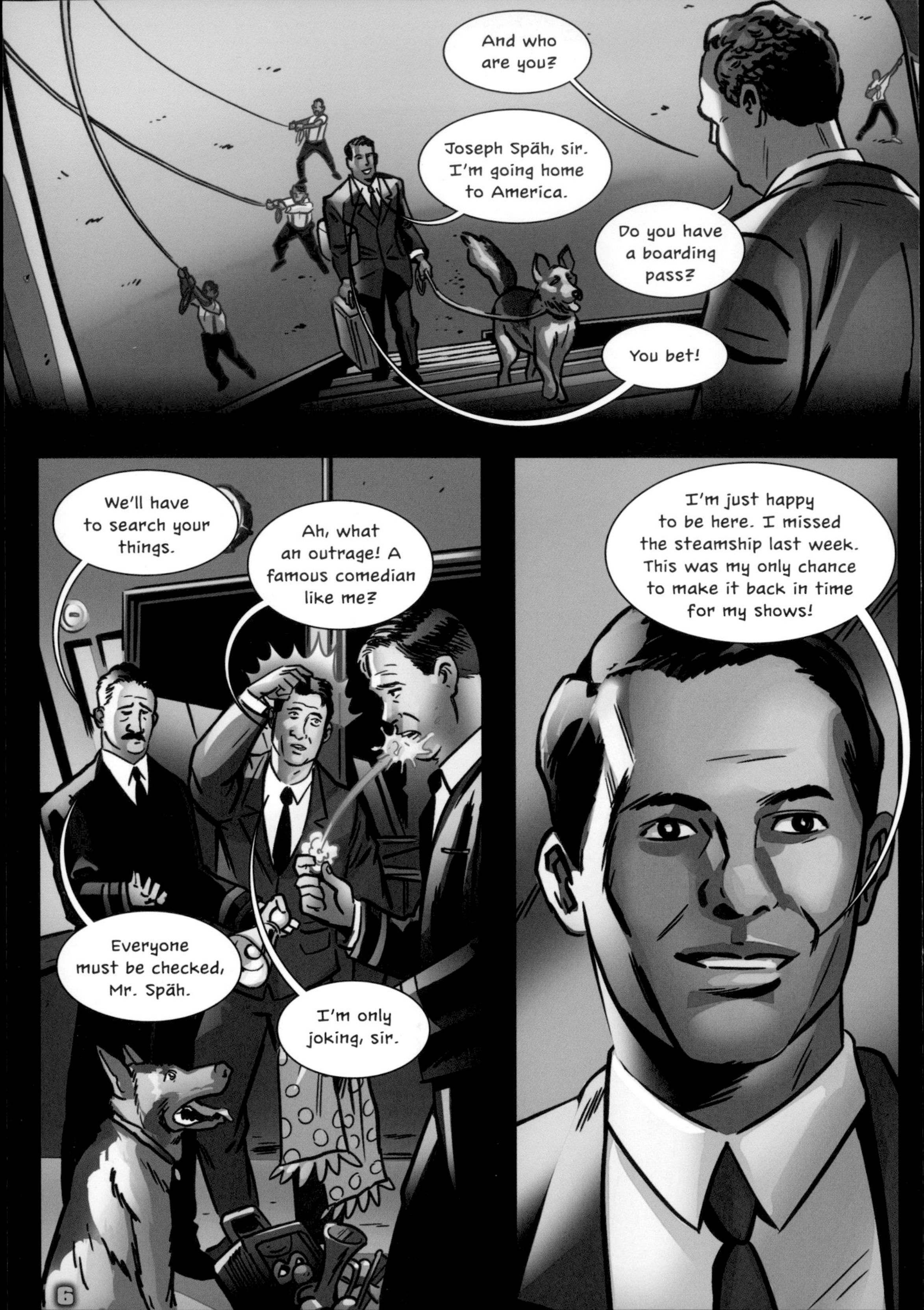
And who are you?
Joseph Späh, sir. I'm going home to America.
Do you have a boarding pass?
You bet!
We'll have to search your things.
Ah, what an outrage! A famous comedian like me?
Everyone must be checked, Mr. Späh.
I'm only joking, sir.
I'm just happy to be here. I missed the steamship last week. This was my only chance to make it back in time for my shows!

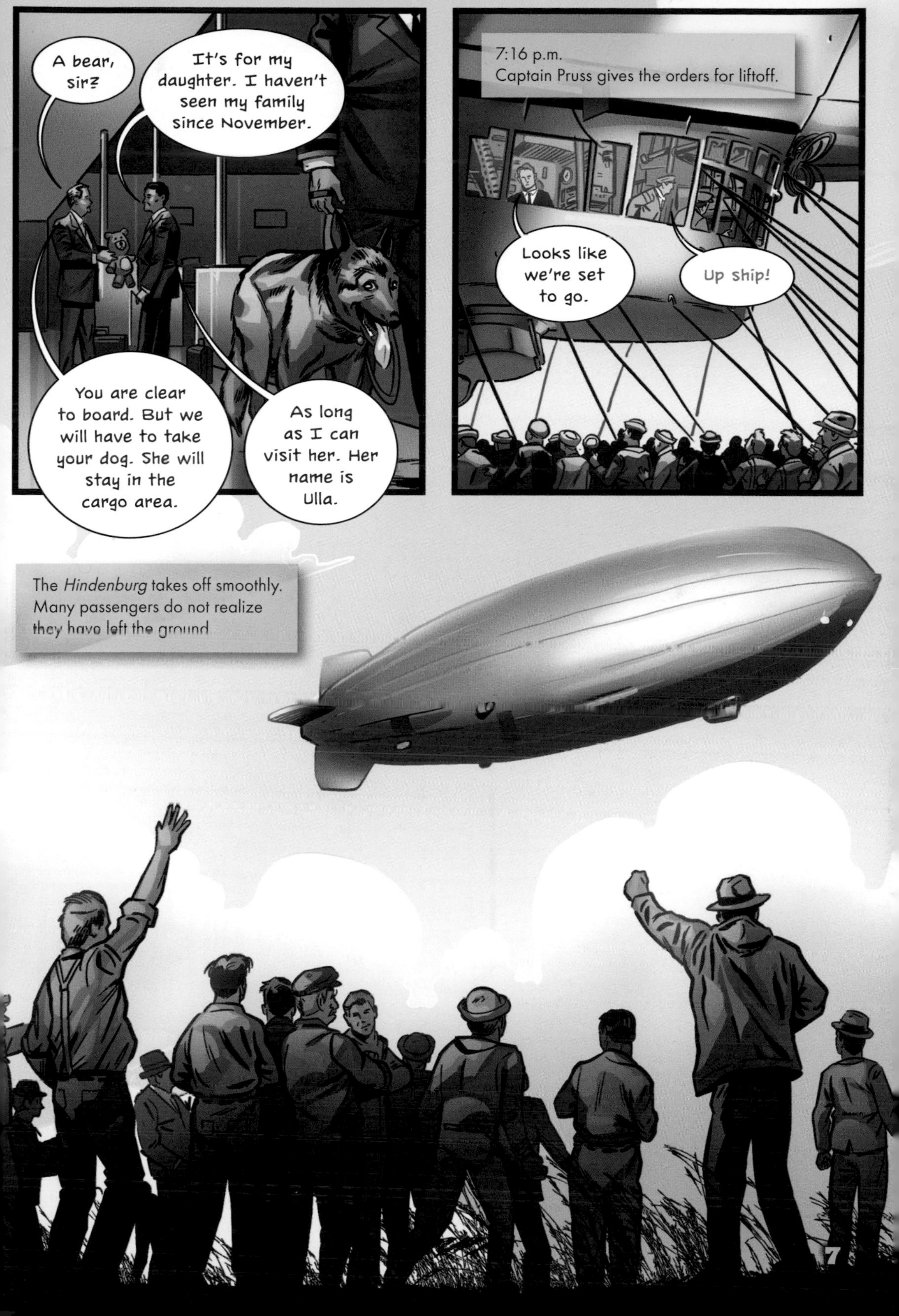
A bear, sir?
It's for my daughter. I haven't seen my family since November.
You are clear to board. But we will have to take your dog. She will stay in the cargo area.
As long as I can visit her. Her name is Ulla.
7:16 p.m.
Captain Pruss gives the orders for liftoff.
Looks like we're set to go.
Up ship!
The *Hindenburg* takes off smoothly. Many passengers do not realize they have left the ground.

Traveling in Style

The *Hindenburg* takes a northern route over the Atlantic Ocean. From Germany, it flies over the Netherlands and southern England.

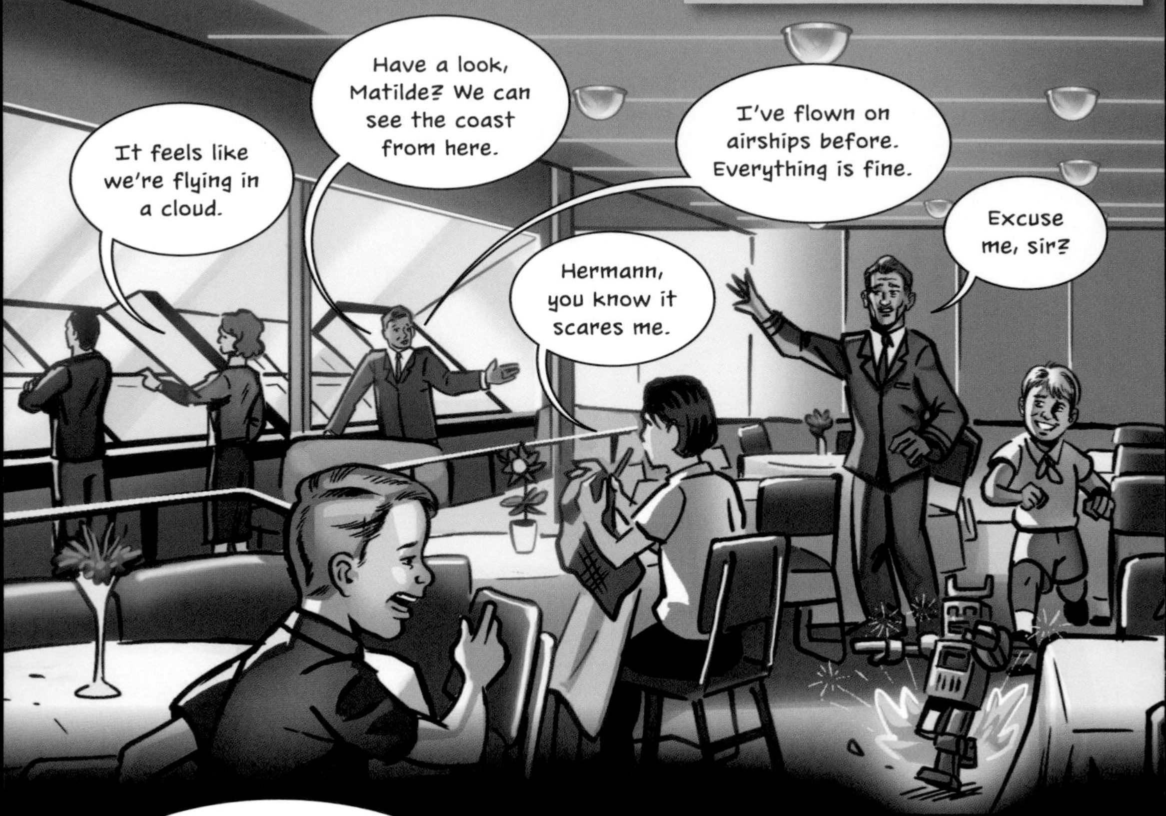
It feels like we're flying in a cloud.
Have a look, Matilde? We can see the coast from here.
I've flown on airships before. Everything is fine.
Hermann, you know it scares me.
Excuse me, sir?

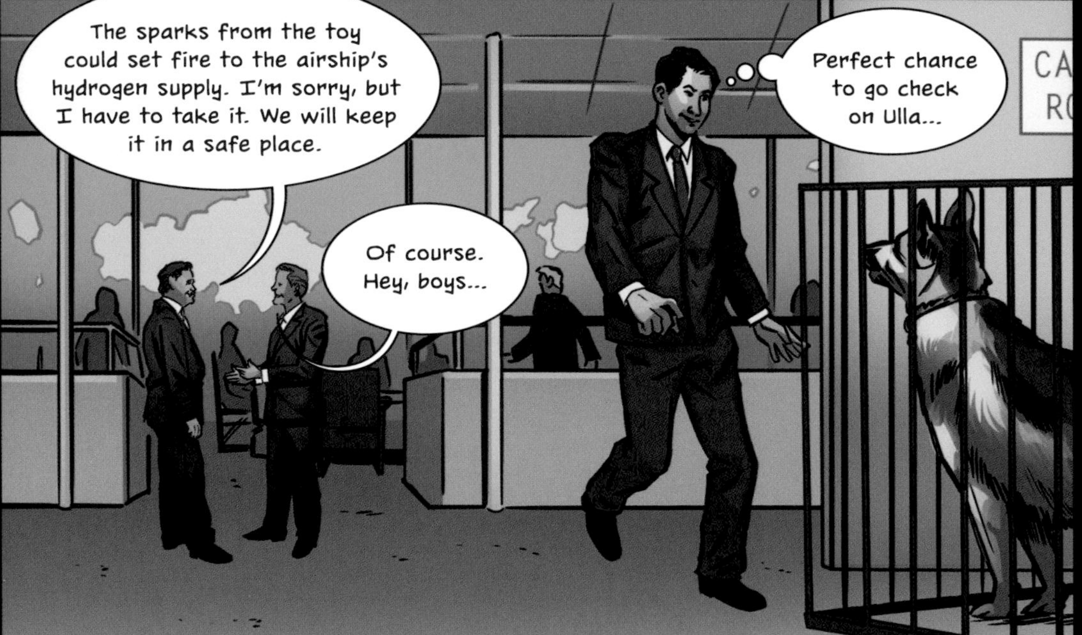
The sparks from the toy could set fire to the airship's hydrogen supply. I'm sorry, but I have to take it. We will keep it in a safe place.
Of course. Hey, boys...
Perfect chance to go check on Ulla...

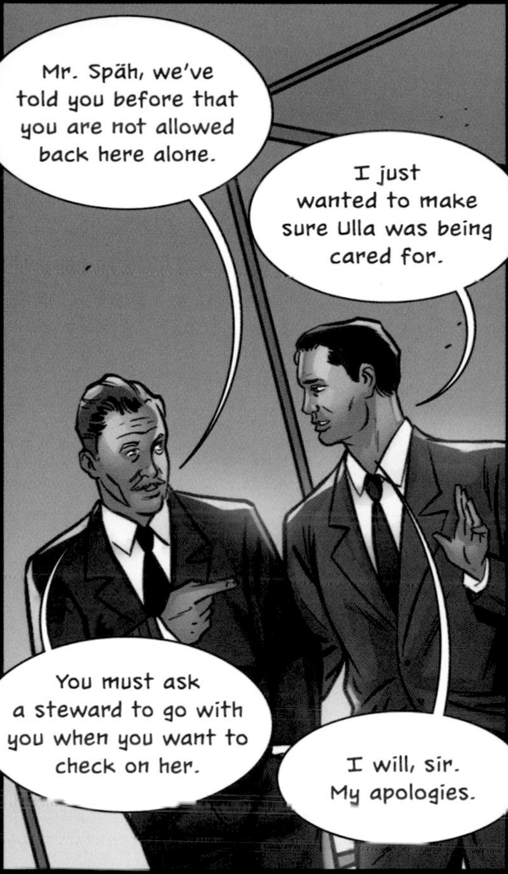
Mr. Späh, we've told you before that you are not allowed back here alone.
I just wanted to make sure Ulla was being cared for.
You must ask a steward to go with you when you want to check on her.
I will, sir. My apologies.

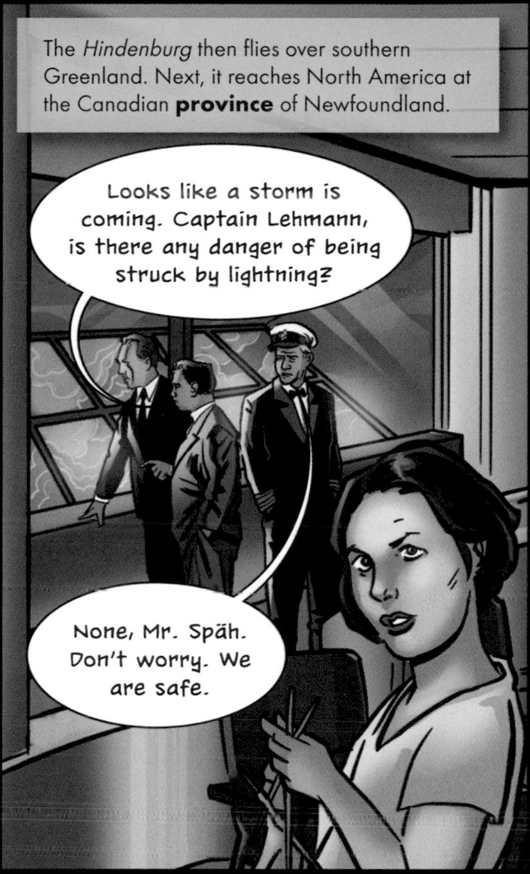
The *Hindenburg* then flies over southern Greenland. Next, it reaches North America at the Canadian **province** of Newfoundland.
Looks like a storm is coming. Captain Lehmann, is there any danger of being struck by lightning?
None, Mr. Späh. Don't worry. We are safe.

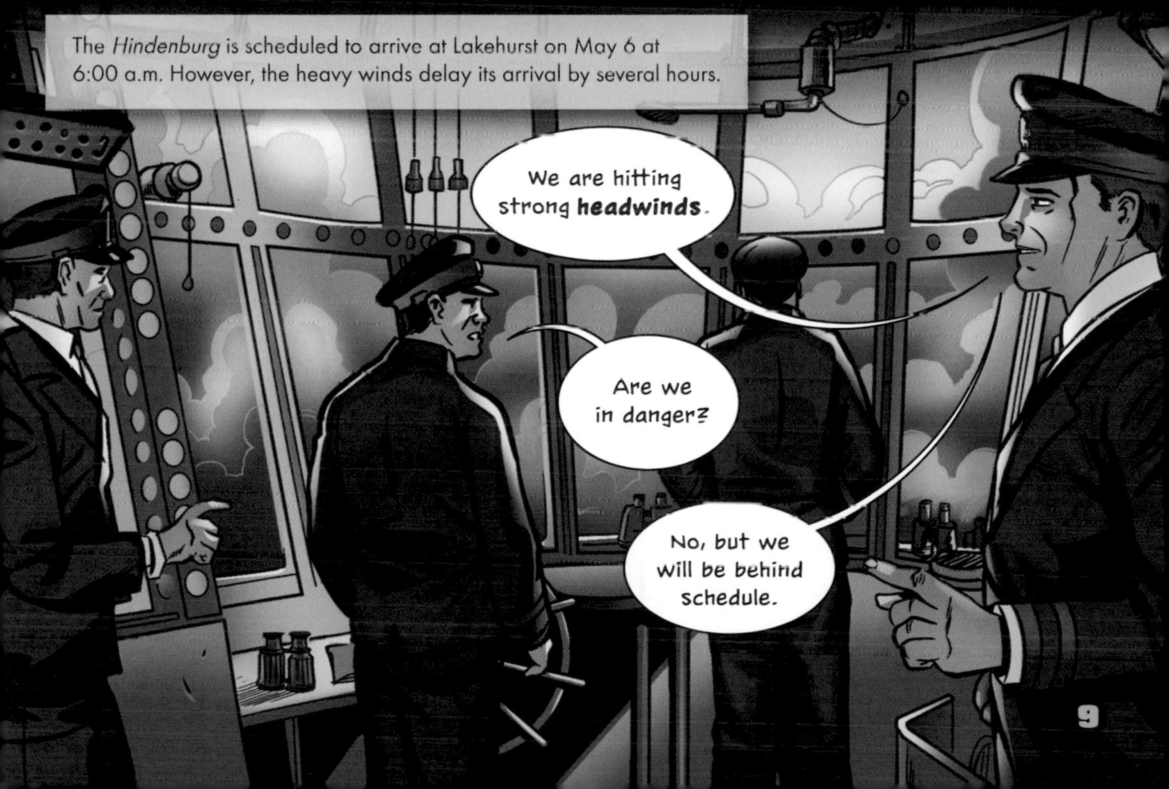
The *Hindenburg* is scheduled to arrive at Lakehurst on May 6 at 6:00 a.m. However, the heavy winds delay its arrival by several hours.
We are hitting strong **headwinds**.
Are we in danger?
No, but we will be behind schedule.

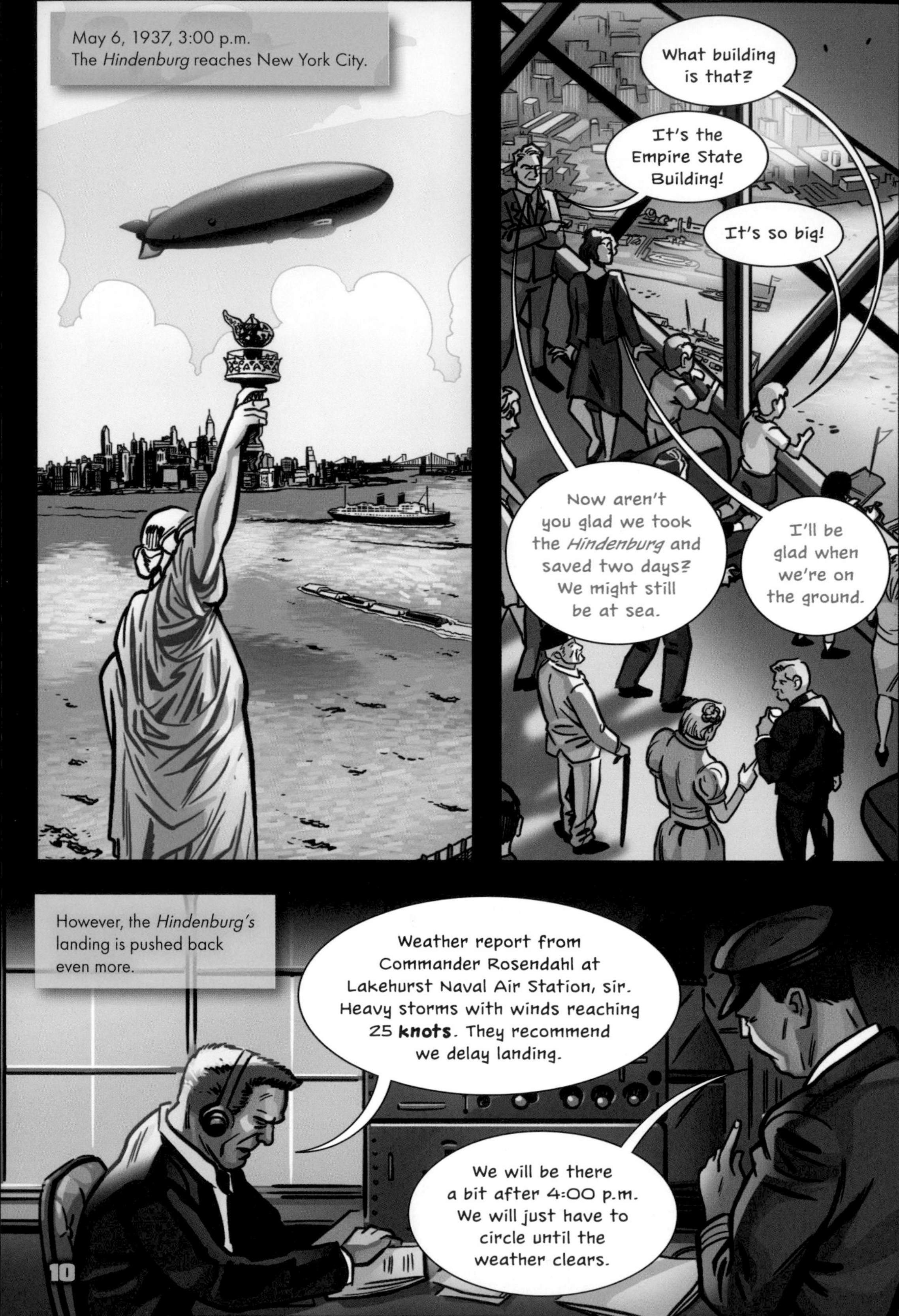
May 6, 1937, 3:00 p.m.
The *Hindenburg* reaches New York City.
What building is that?
It's the Empire State Building!
It's so big!
Now aren't you glad we took the *Hindenburg* and saved two days? We might still be at sea.
I'll be glad when we're on the ground.
However, the *Hindenburg's* landing is pushed back even more.
Weather report from Commander Rosendahl at Lakehurst Naval Air Station, sir. Heavy storms with winds reaching 25 **knots**. They recommend we delay landing.
We will be there a bit after 4:00 p.m. We will just have to circle until the weather clears.

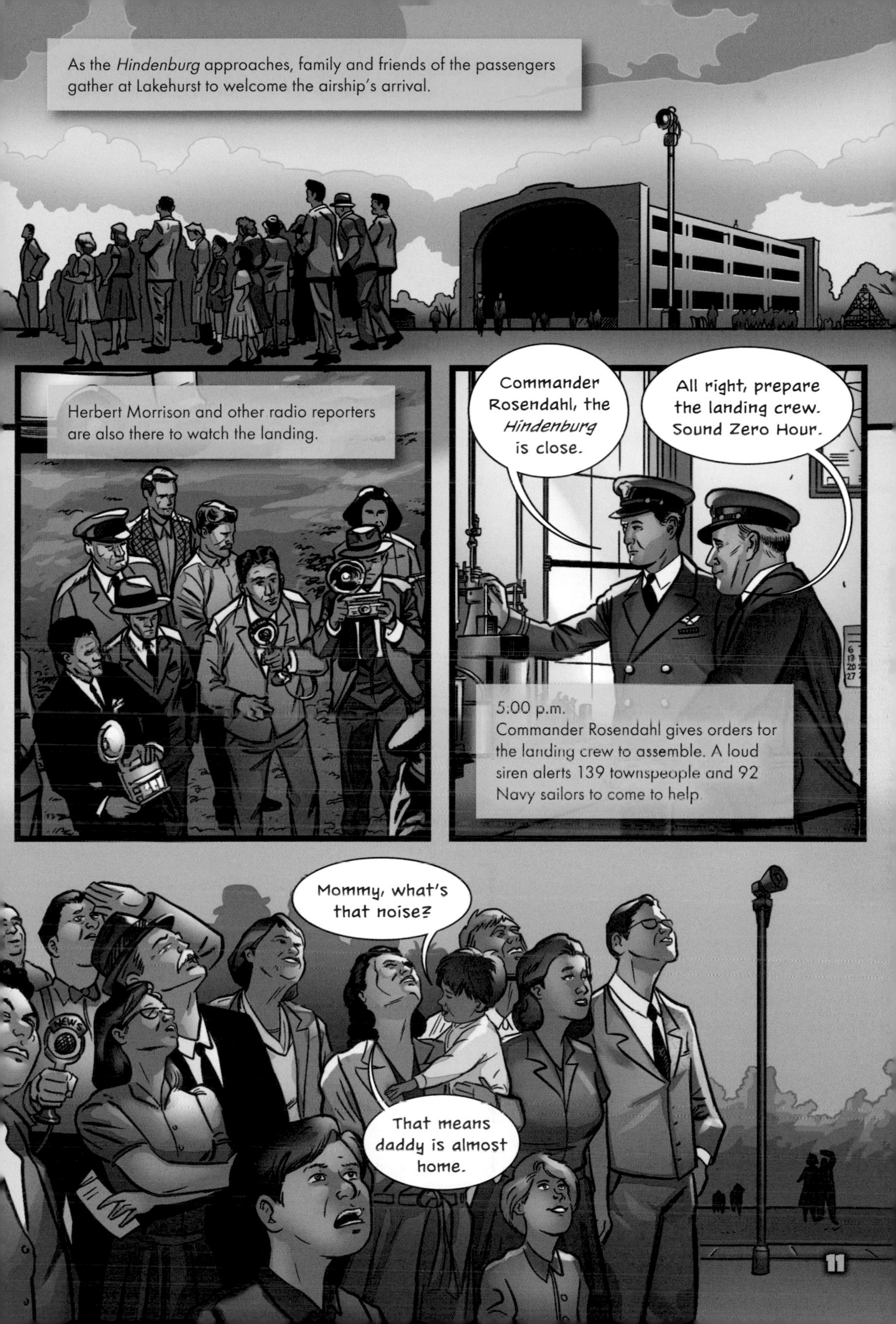
As the *Hindenburg* approaches, family and friends of the passengers gather at Lakehurst to welcome the airship's arrival.
Herbert Morrison and other radio reporters are also there to watch the landing.
Commander Rosendahl, the *Hindenburg* is close.
All right, prepare the landing crew. Sound Zero Hour.
5:00 p.m.
Commander Rosendahl gives orders for the landing crew to assemble. A loud siren alerts 139 townspeople and 92 Navy sailors to come to help.
Mommy, what's that noise?
That means daddy is almost home.
NEWS

6:00 p.m.
It is raining too hard to land the *Hindenburg*.
Passengers grow frustrated as they look out
the windows.

What is taking
so long?

We have to
wait for better
weather.

6:12 p.m.
The weather begins to clear.

Conditions
now considered
suitable for
landing.

Just after 7:00 p.m.
The *Hindenburg* returns to Lakehurst to land.
The airship circles the area to lower its **altitude**.

Conditions
definitely improved,
recommend earliest
possible landing.

I'm reducing
the engines.
Officer Sammt,
lower us down.

We will have
to balance out
before dropping
the lines.

Officer Sammt releases some of the
hydrogen from the tanks. He also drops
over 2,420 pounds of **ballast water**
from the tail of the ship.

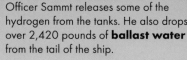

We seem
to be level
now, sir.

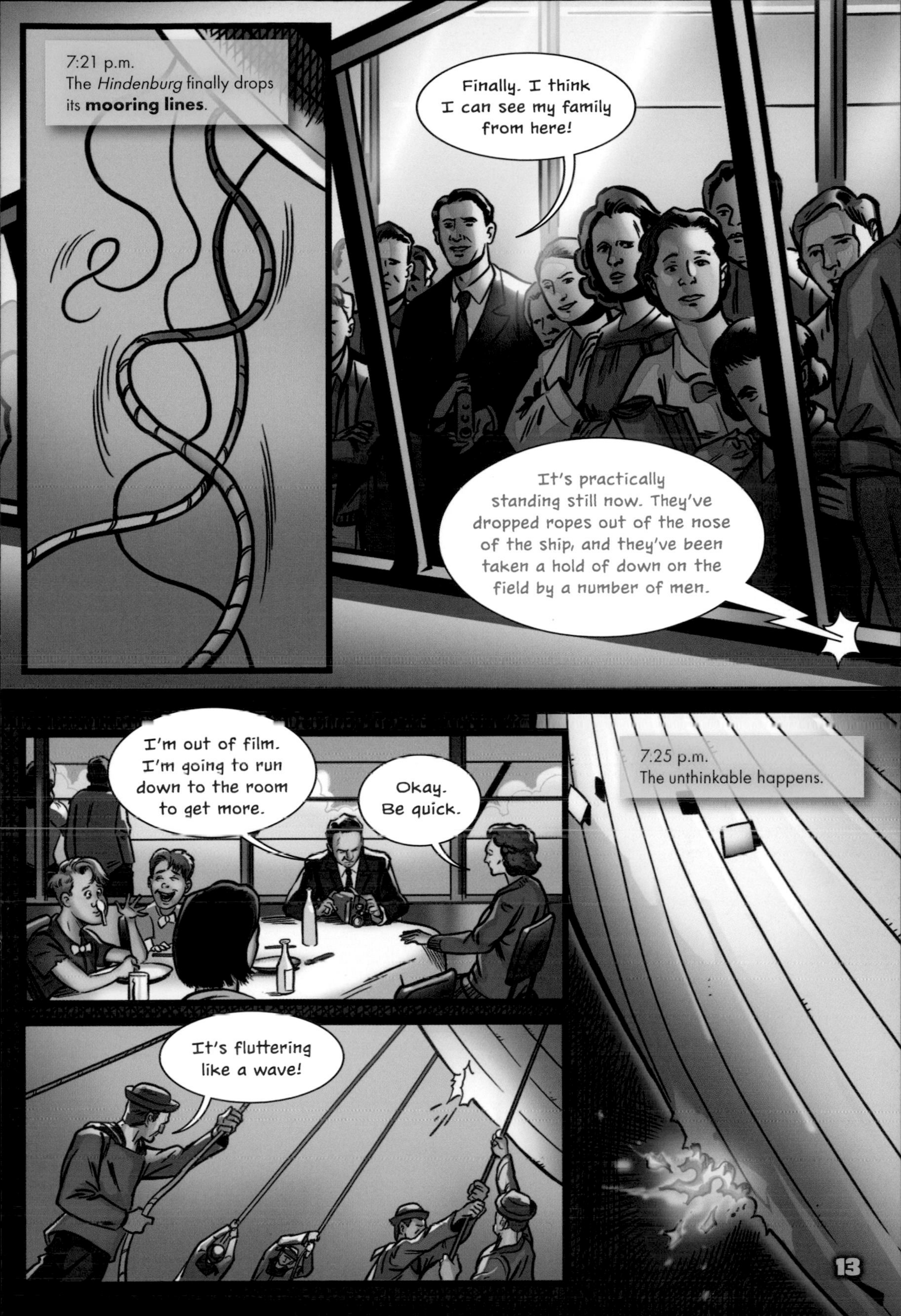
7:21 p.m.
The *Hindenburg* finally drops its **mooring lines**.
Finally. I think I can see my family from here!
It's practically standing still now. They've dropped ropes out of the nose of the ship, and they've been taken a hold of down on the field by a number of men.
I'm out of film. I'm going to run down to the room to get more.
Okay. Be quick.
It's fluttering like a wave!
7:25 p.m.
The unthinkable happens.

Disaster Strikes!

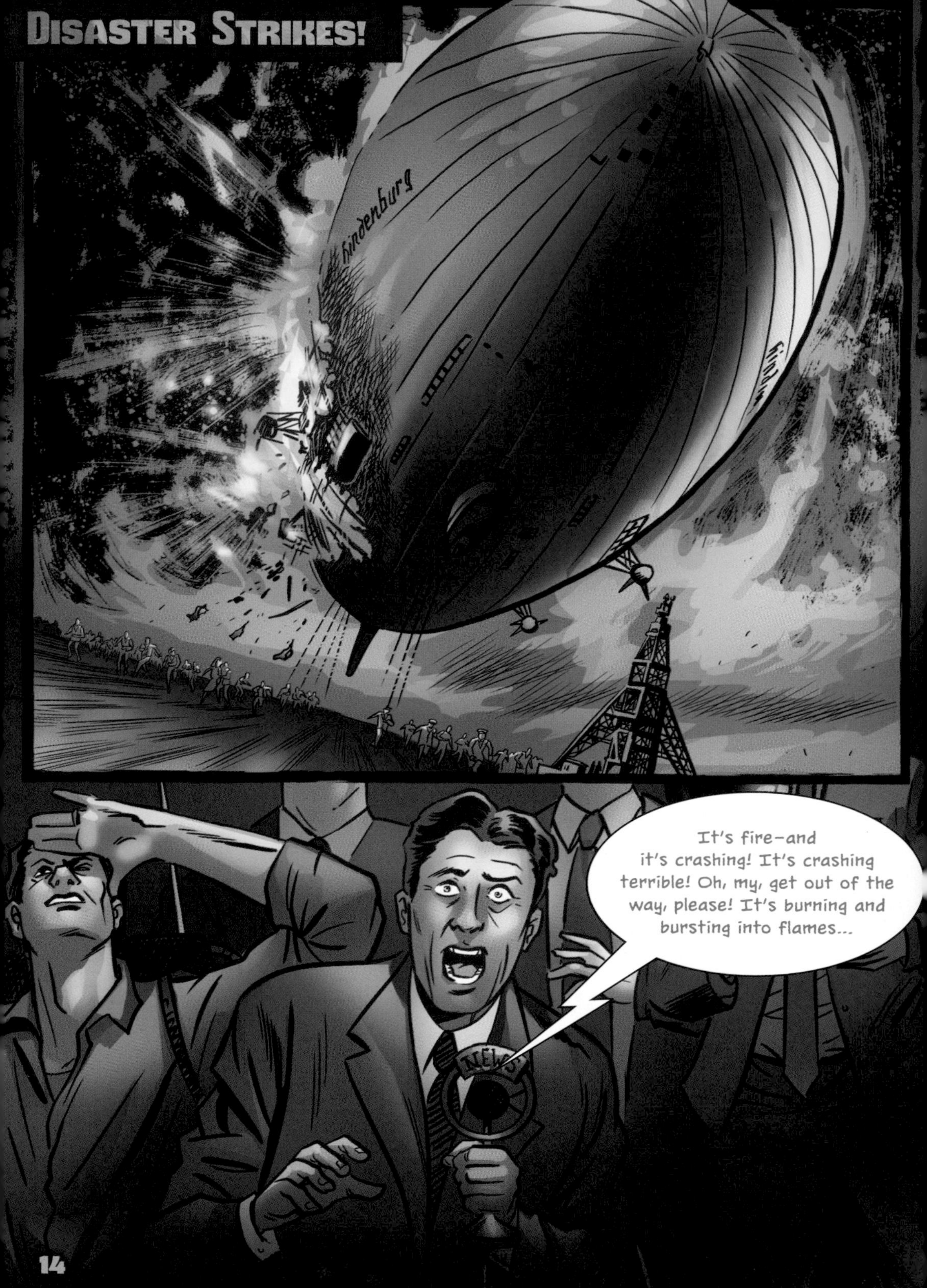
Hindenburg
NEWS
It's fire—and it's crashing! It's crashing terrible! Oh, my, get out of the way, please! It's burning and bursting into flames...

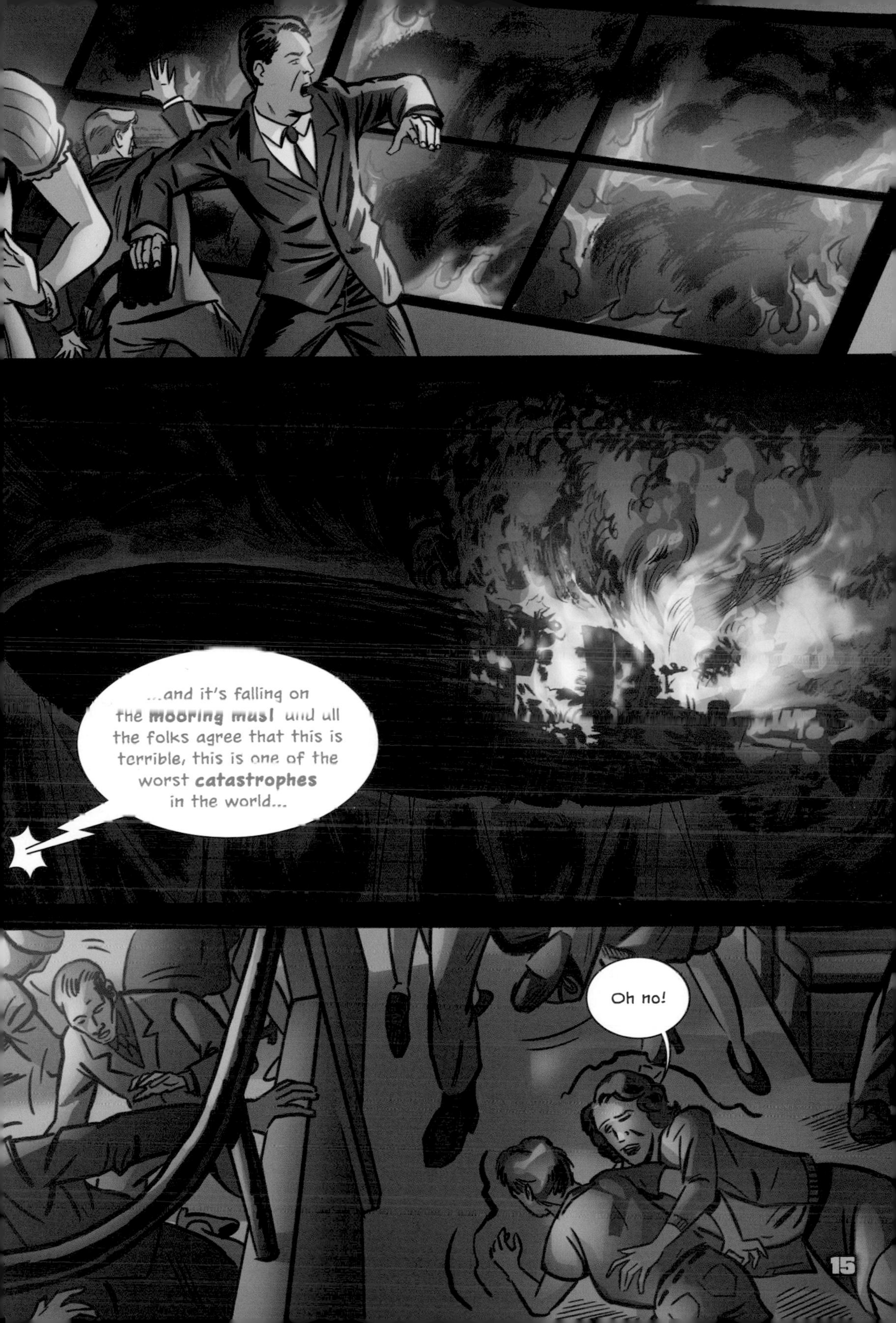
...and it's falling on the mooring mast and all the folks agree that this is terrible, this is one of the worst catastrophes in the world...
Oh no!

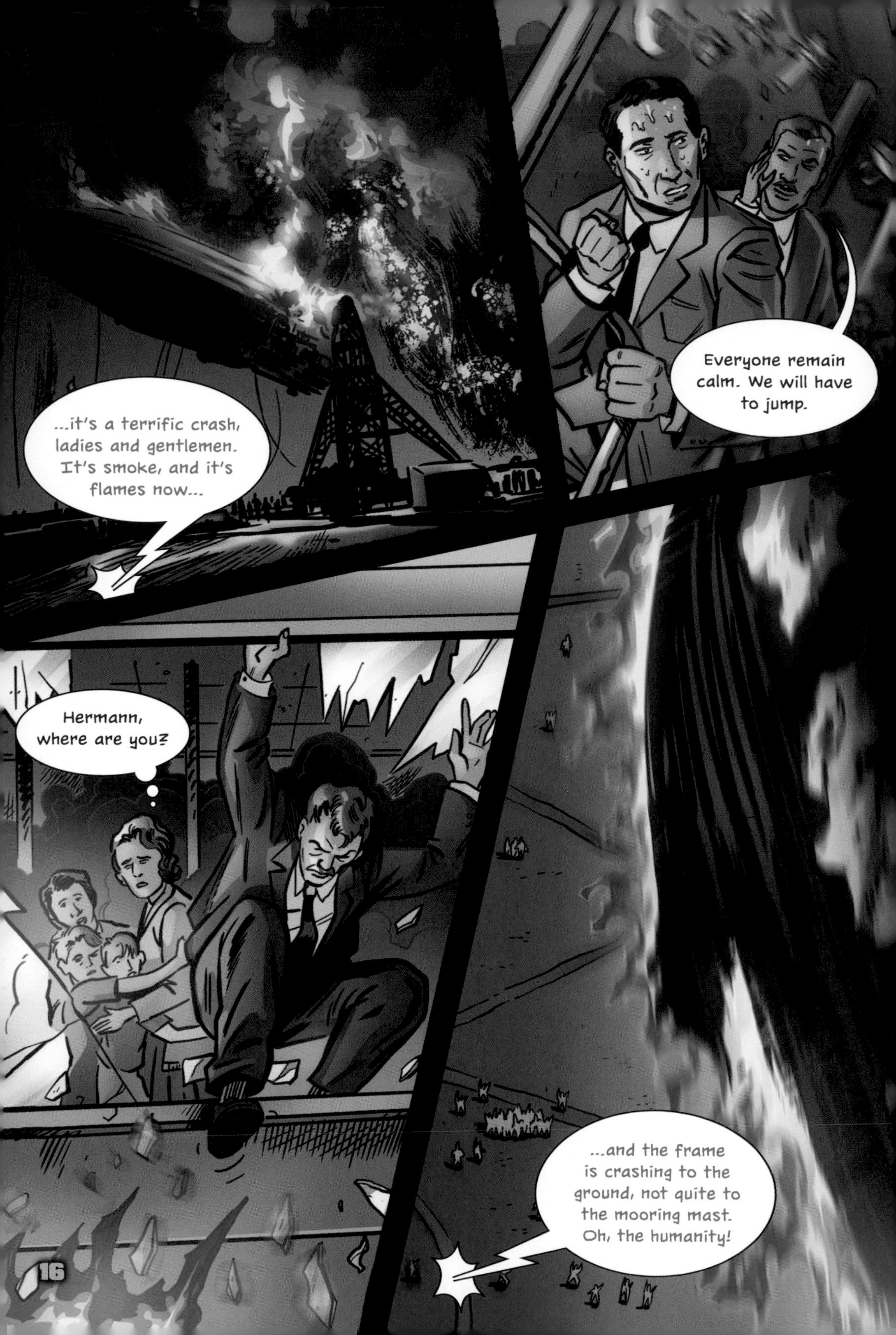
...it's a terrific crash, ladies and gentlemen. It's smoke, and it's flames now...
Everyone remain calm. We will have to jump.
Hermann, where are you?
...and the frame is crashing to the ground, not quite to the mooring mast. Oh, the humanity!

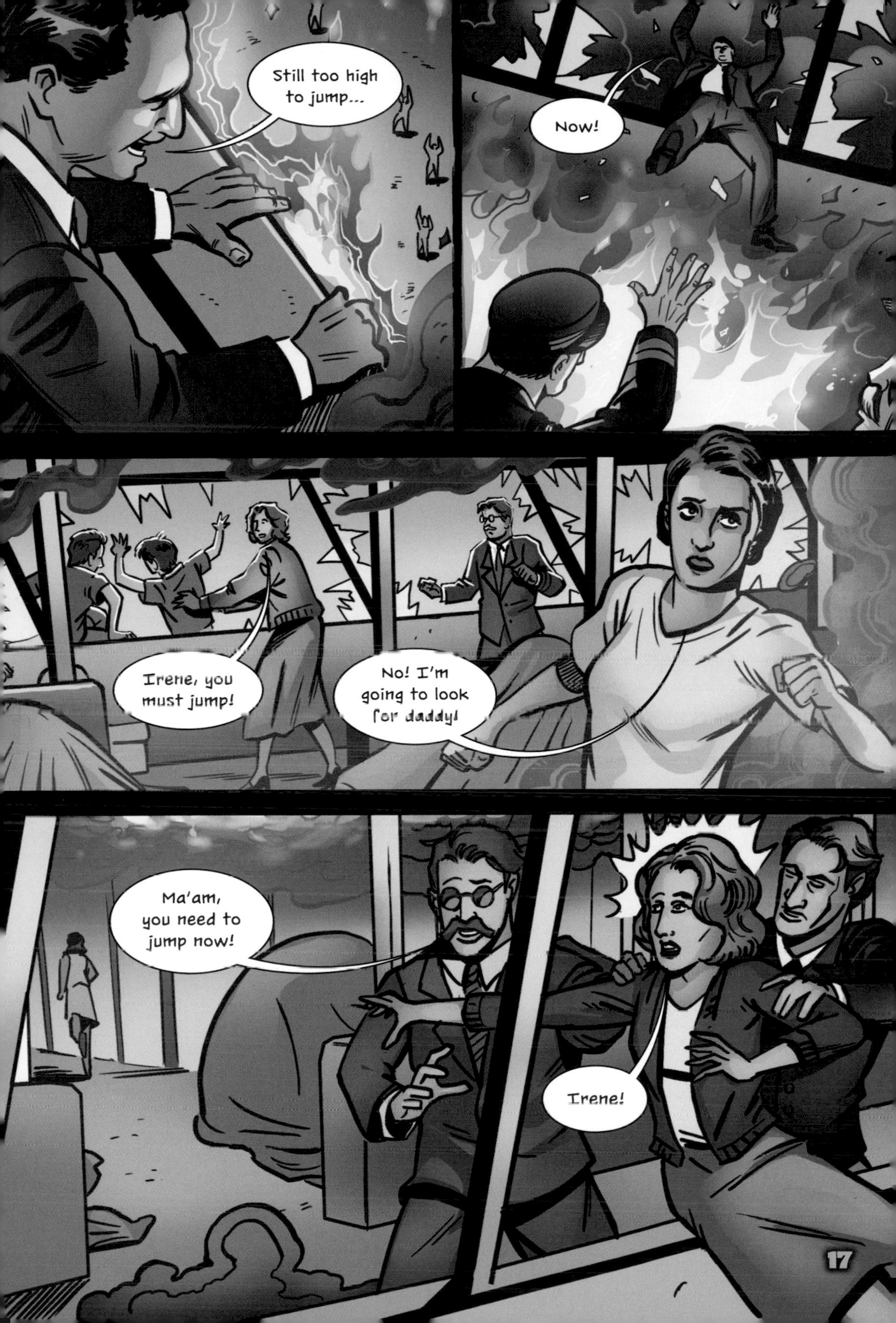
Still too high to jump...
Now!
Irene, you must jump!
No! I'm going to look for daddy!
Ma'am, you need to jump now!
Irene!

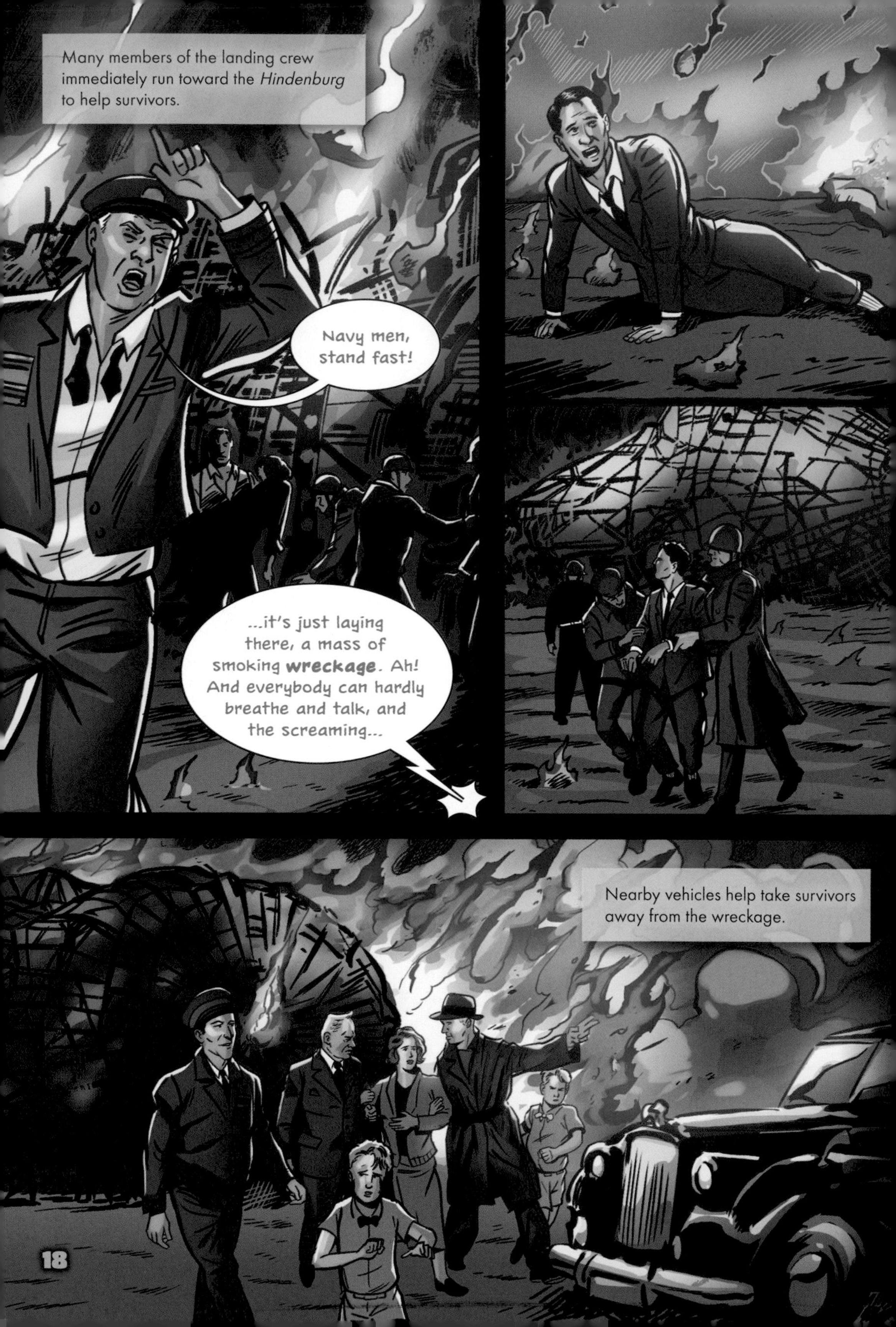
Many members of the landing crew immediately run toward the *Hindenburg* to help survivors.
Navy men, stand fast!
...it's just laying there, a mass of smoking **wreckage**. Ah! And everybody can hardly breathe and talk, and the screaming...
Nearby vehicles help take survivors away from the wreckage.

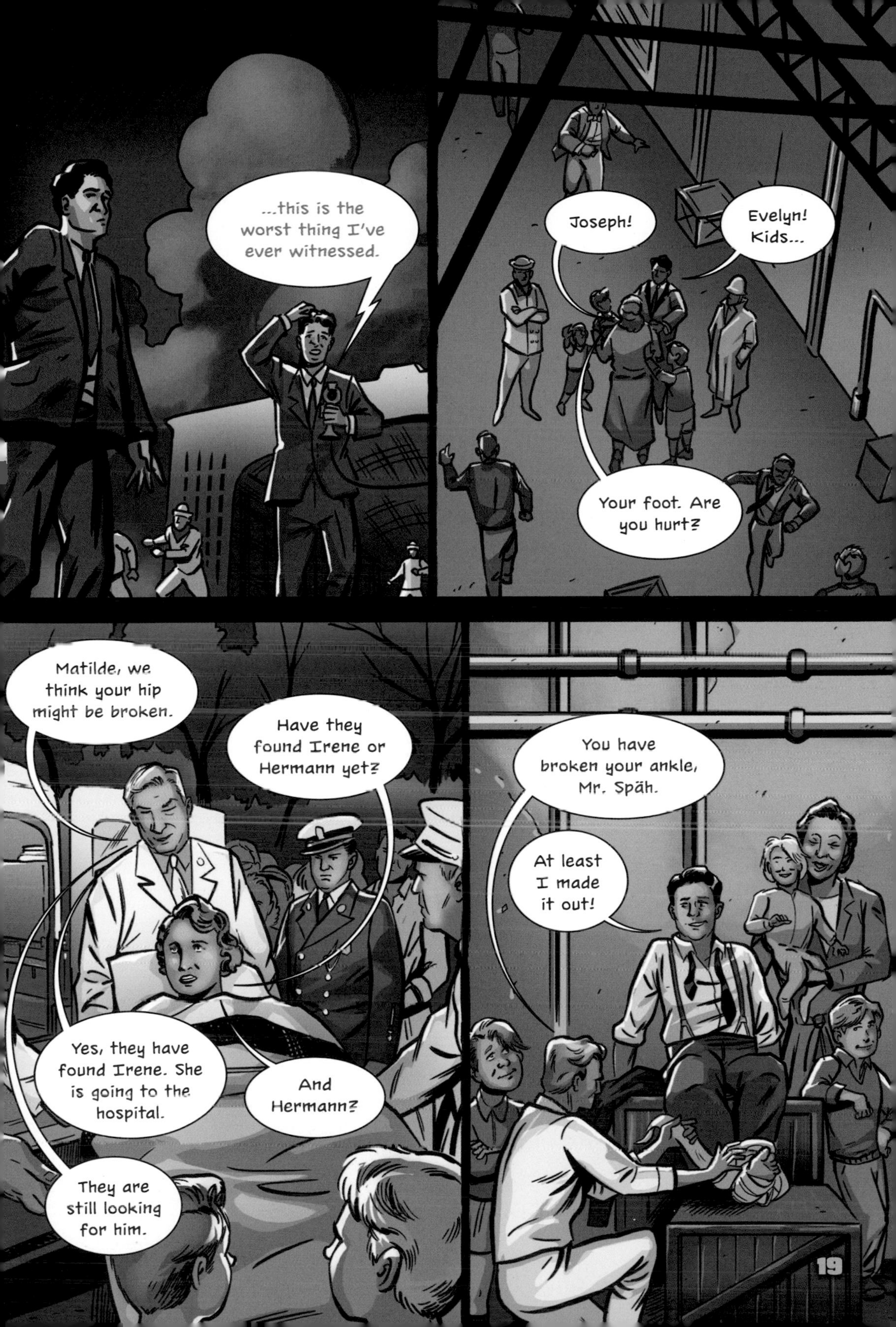

...this is the worst thing I've ever witnessed.
Joseph!
Evelyn! Kids...
Your foot. Are you hurt?
Matilde, we think your hip might be broken.
Have they found Irene or Hermann yet?
Yes, they have found Irene. She is going to the hospital.
And Hermann?
They are still looking for him.
You have broken your ankle, Mr. Späh.
At least I made it out!

THE AFTERMATH

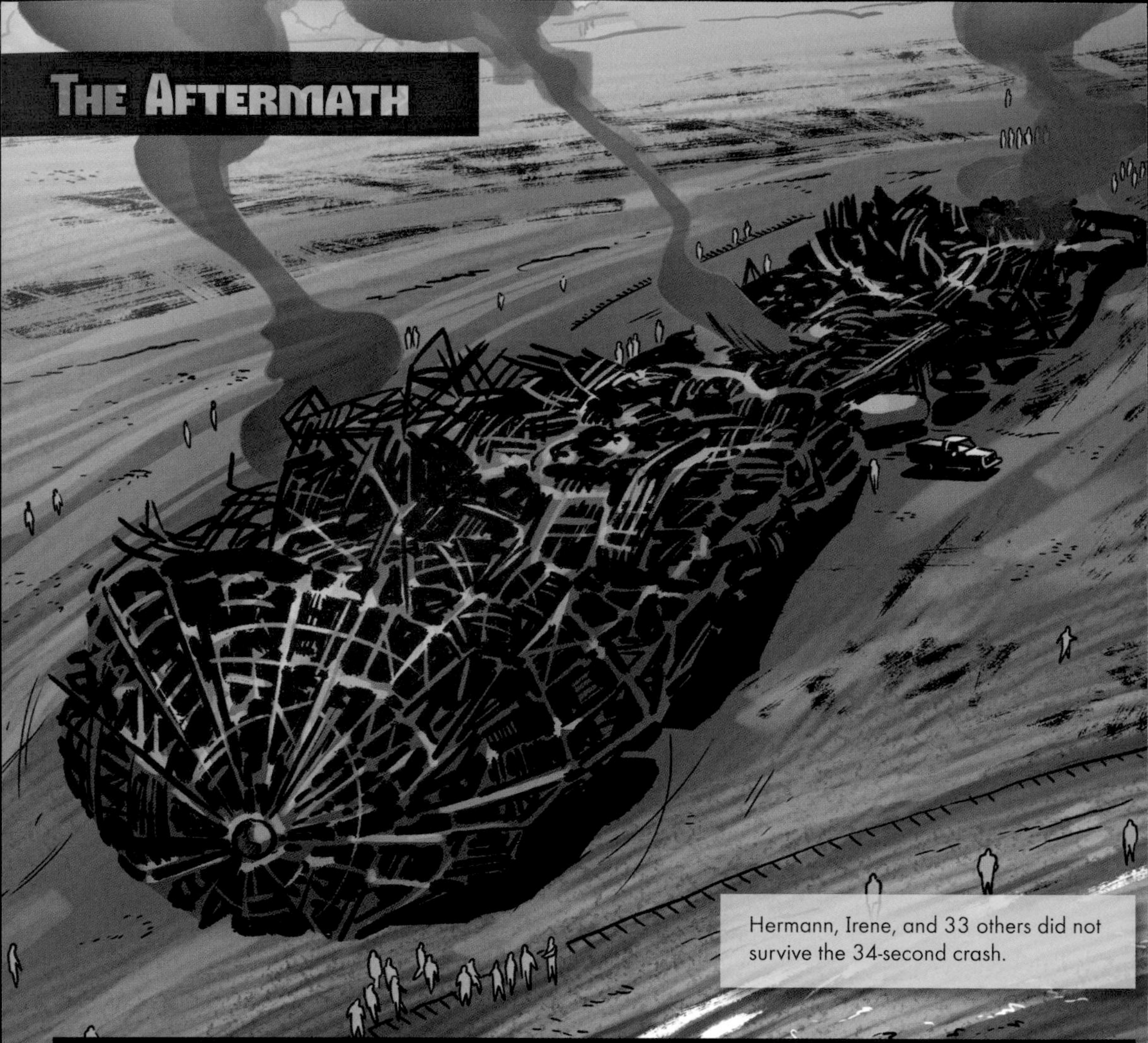
Hermann, Irene, and 33 others did not survive the 34-second crash.

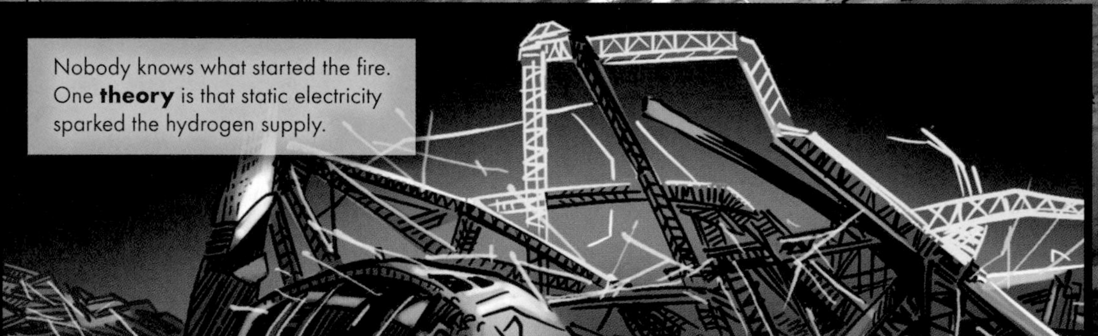
Nobody knows what started the fire. One **theory** is that static electricity sparked the hydrogen supply.

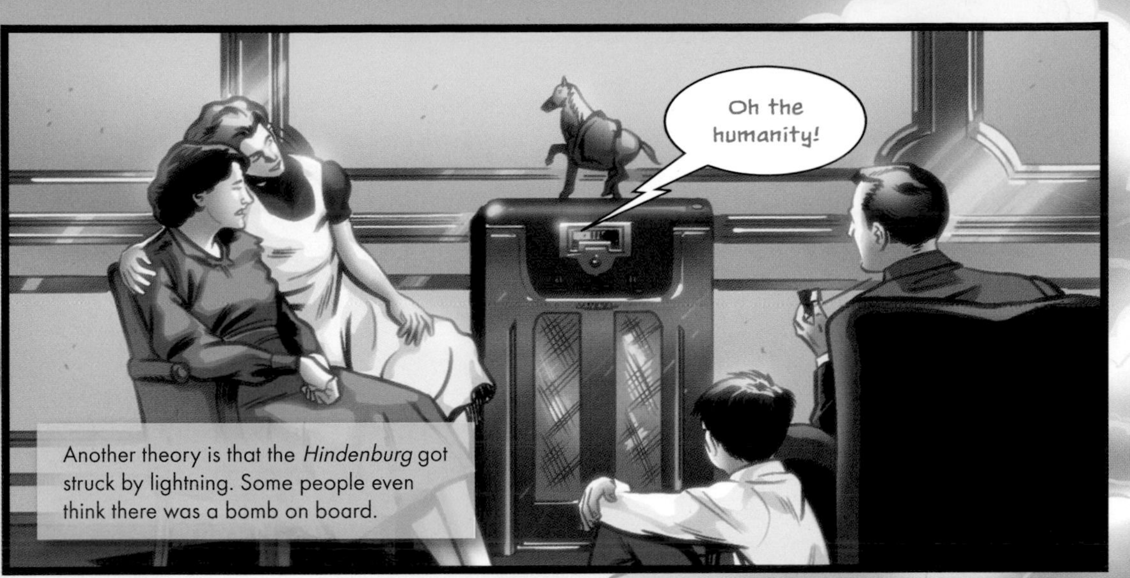
Oh the humanity!
Another theory is that the *Hindenburg* got struck by lightning. Some people even think there was a bomb on board.

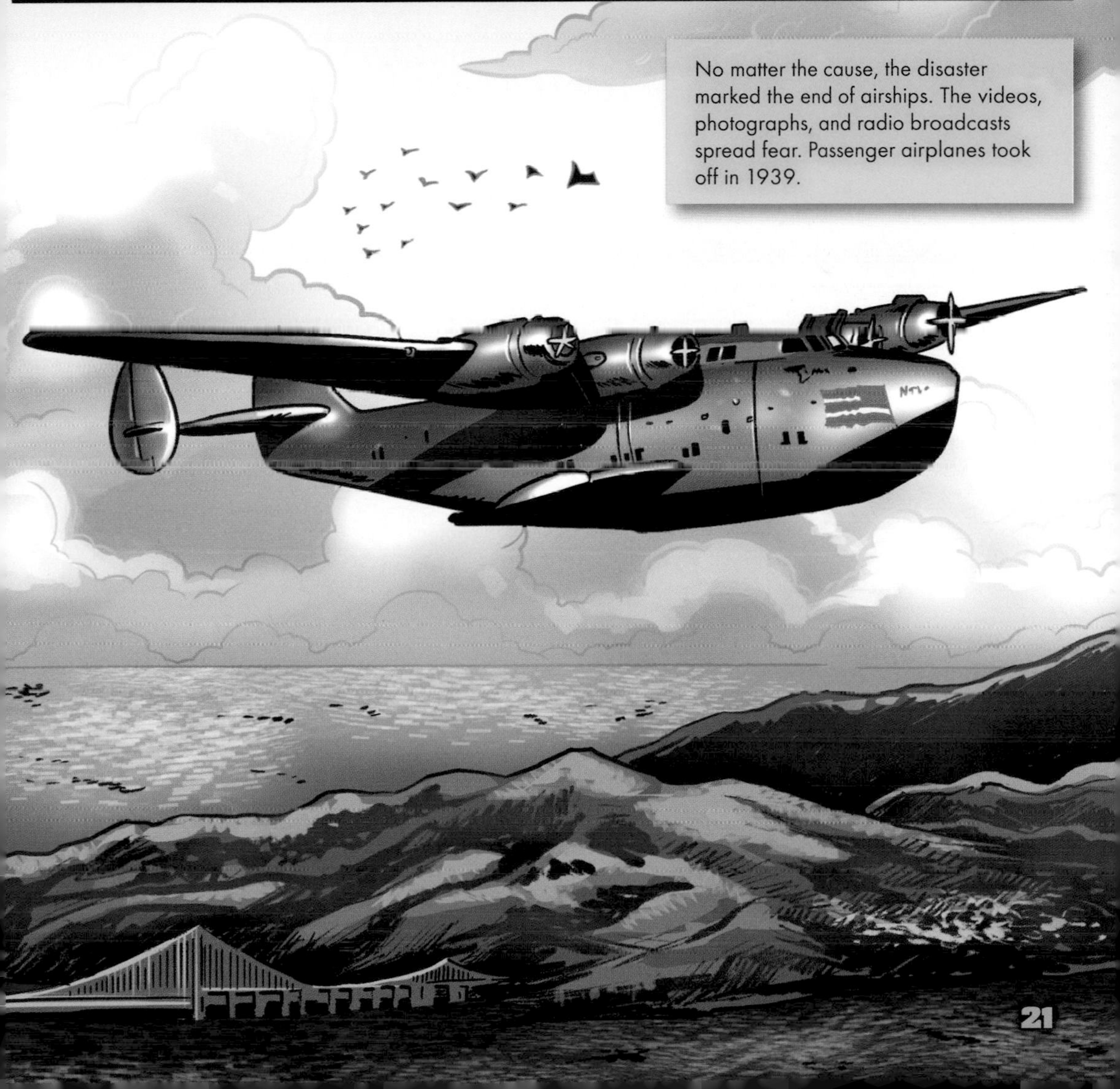
No matter the cause, the disaster marked the end of airships. The videos, photographs, and radio broadcasts spread fear. Passenger airplanes took off in 1939.

More About the Disaster

- Airships were also known as *dirigibles* or *zeppelins*.

- Throughout 1936, the *Hindenburg* had a baby grand piano in one of the lounges. It was made of aluminum to keep it light. It was taken out before 1937 to save weight.

- The *Hindenburg* was carrying about 17,000 letters on its trip to the U.S. About 170 of these survived the crash and were delivered.

- Herbert Morrison's report of the *Hindenburg* disaster was not broadcast live on the radio. The recording was played the next day.

- Instead of hydrogen, the *Hindenburg* was designed to use helium, which was less capable of catching fire. However, the U.S. controlled the world's helium supply. They did not sell any to Germany out of fear that it would be used for military purposes.

Glossary

airship—a large aircraft filled with a lighter-than-air gas

altitude—the height above ground

ballast water—water kept in an airship to keep it stable and control its height

catastrophes—sudden disasters or tragedies

headwinds—winds blowing against the direction of travel

knots—a way to measure the speed of aircraft and ships; a knot is equal to one nautical mile, or 1.15 miles (1.85 kilometers).

luxury travel—comfortable ways for the upper class to move from place to place

mooring lines—ropes used to keep an airship in place; workers used mooring lines to help airships land.

mooring mast—a structure that airships use to land; airships dock at mooring masts.

promenades—open areas with windows for passengers to look out

province—an area within a country; provinces are similar to states.

steamships—ships powered by a steam engine

theory—an idea that tries to explain something

wreckage—the remains of something that has been badly damaged or destroyed

To Learn More

AT THE LIBRARY

Berne, Emma Carlson. *The Rescue Adventure of Stenny Green, Hindenburg Crash Eyewitness*. Minneapolis, Minn.: Graphic Universe, 2011.

Doeden, Matt. *The Hindenburg Disaster*. Mankato, Minn.: Capstone Press, 2006.

Gunderson, Jessica. *Fire in the Sky: A Tale of the Hindenburg Explosion*. Mankato, Minn.: Stone Arch Books, 2009.

ON THE WEB

Learning more about the *Hindenburg* disaster is as easy as 1, 2, 3.

1. Go to www.factsurfer.com.
2. Enter "Hindenburg disaster" into the search box.
3. Click the "Surf" button and you will see a list of related web sites.

With factsurfer.com, finding more information is just a click away.

Index